Who Was
Marco Polo?

Who Was
Marco Polo?

By Joan Holub
Illustrated by John O'Brien

Grosset & Dunlap

For George Hallowell, who makes traveling fun—J.H.

For Linda—J.O.B.

GROSSET & DUNLAP
Published by the Penguin Group
Penguin Group (USA) Inc., 375 Hudson Street, New York, New York 10014, U.S.A.
Penguin Group (Canada), 90 Eglinton Avenue East, Suite 700, Toronto,
Ontario, Canada M4P 2Y3 (a division of Pearson Penguin Canada Inc.)
Penguin Books Ltd, 80 Strand, London WC2R 0RL, England
Penguin Ireland, 25 St Stephen's Green, Dublin 2, Ireland (a division of Penguin Books Ltd)
Penguin Group (Australia), 250 Camberwell Road,
Camberwell, Victoria 3124, Australia (a division of Pearson Australia Group Pty Ltd)
Penguin Books India Pvt Ltd, 11 Community Centre,
Panchsheel Park, New Delhi—110 017, India
Penguin Group (NZ), 67 Apollo Drive, Mairangi Bay, Auckland 1311,
New Zealand (a division of Pearson New Zealand Ltd)
Penguin Books (South Africa) (Pty) Ltd, 24 Sturdee Avenue,
Rosebank, Johannesburg 2196, South Africa

Penguin Books Ltd, Registered Offices: 80 Strand, London WC2R 0RL, England

Text copyright © 2007 by Joan Holub. Illustrations copyright © 2007 by John O'Brien.
Cover illustration copyright © 2007 by Nancy Harrison. All rights reserved.
Published by Grosset & Dunlap, a division of Penguin Young Readers Group,
345 Hudson Street, New York, New York 10014.
GROSSET & DUNLAP is a trademark of Penguin Group (USA) Inc.
Printed in the U.S.A.

Library of Congress Control Number: 2006038243

ISBN 978-0-448-44540-3   10 9 8 7 6 5 4 3 2 1

Contents

Who Was
Marco Polo?

MARCO POLO

Marco Polo lived in Venice, Italy, more than seven hundred fifty years ago. Back then, in the 1200s, most people spent their whole lives right where they were born. But not Marco. He made an eleven-thousand-mile trip to China and back. And he became the most famous traveler in Europe. Not just because he made such a long and dangerous trip (although hardly anyone else in Europe had done this at the time), but because he wrote a book about his adventure.

Like his father and uncle, Marco was a merchant. The Polos wanted to go to Asia to bring back silk, spices, and other expensive goods to sell in Europe. Marco was a teenager when he went off to China. He didn't return to Italy for twenty-four years!

China's ruler was named Kublai Kahn (KOO-bluh kahn). He liked Marco and sent him to nearby countries to spy. Marco took notes about the places he saw and the customs of the people he met. He used these notes to write a book about his travels.

Reading his book was the way many Europeans learned about Asia.

CHRISTOPHER COLUMBUS

Two hundred years later, explorers such as Christopher Columbus and Vasco de Gama read Marco's book. It made them want to reach Asia, too. But they hoped to find an easier route.

Was everything in Marco's book true? Historians think he exaggerated here and there. Some even think he never went to China at all. Still, his book made him famous around the world.

What is the true story of Marco Polo?

Chapter 1
A Family of Merchants

Two things made the year 1254 important in Marco Polo's life. First, it was the year he was born. And second, it was the year his father, who was named Niccolo, and his uncle Maffeo left Venice on a trading trip to Asia. Marco's father was gone so long that Marco was fifteen years old when they met for the first time!

Soon after Marco was born, his mother died. He was sent to live with relatives. As a boy, he didn't spend much time in school. Instead, his family taught him things he needed to know to become a merchant.

For instance, Venetians used coins such as silver grossos and gold ducats (DUK-ets). Marco needed to know how to weigh the coins correctly.

A HOUSE IN VENICE

Venetians had their own measuring system. It was based on using their hands and feet. For instance, one palm was about nine and a half inches. Cloth would have been measured in

palms. Other countries used different kinds of money and measurements. Marco needed to learn about them, too. Otherwise, merchants could cheat him.

The sailors and merchants Marco met on Venice's docks also taught him about trading. Venice was the most powerful trading city in the world. Its busy port, with ships constantly coming and going, was on the Adriatic Sea.

Venice was not like most cities. It was actually a group of 118 tiny islands connected by canals.

Marco and his family traveled the canals in long canoelike boats called gondolas (GAHN-doh-lahz).

Back then Italy was not a country. It was a group of city-states. Each city-state ruled itself. Venice was one of the largest, with as many as one hundred thousand people.

Venice sold its products—wood, wheat, and salt—to foreign lands. Salt was very valuable in those days. And lots of it washed up on Venice's shores. Since there were no refrigerators, salt was used to keep fish and meat from rotting. Without salt, they rotted within a week. But salted, these foods

could last for months. This was very important on long trips at sea.

While Marco was growing up, his father and uncle kept traveling. By 1260, they were in Constantinople (which is now Istanbul, Turkey). There, they traded the goods they'd brought from Venice. They were paid in jewels.

After crossing the Black Sea, they traveled eastward along the Volga River. In the trading city of Bolgara, they visited a Mongol ruler named Berke Khan. The word *kahn* means "ruler." In return for their jewels, Berke gave the Polos goods worth twice as much. Things were going well.

Unfortunately, a war began between Berke and another Mongol ruler named Hulagu. Both were grandsons of a warlord named Genghis Khan, who had died over thirty years earlier.

The Polos were ready to return home. But the route back to Venice was blocked by the war. Since they couldn't go west, they decided to go east to the city of Bukhara, Uzbekistan. They were trapped there for three years.

Then in 1265, Hulagu sent some messengers to China to visit his brother, Kublai Khan. Kublai and the other khans came from the area marked in stripes on the map—Mongolia. The people of Mongolia were called Mongols.

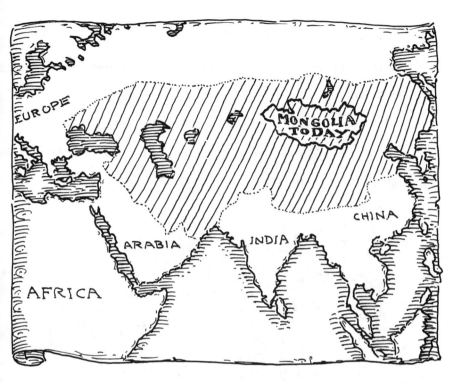

THE MONGOL EMPIRE WAS MUCH BIGGER THAN MONGOLIA IS TODAY. THE STRIPED AREA SHOWS HOW BIG IT WAS BY 1259.

Hulagu's messengers met the Polos and invited them to go along. The Polos agreed. This was a brave decision. Few Europeans had ever been to China, which they called Cathay. Back then, they thought there were only three continents: Europe, Asia, and Africa. They believed that China was at the far end of the world. Bandits, wars, slow transportation, and bad roads made it dangerous to reach.

It took the Polos and the messengers over a year to reach Kublai Khan's palace in the Mongol capital (now Beijing, China). Niccolo

EMPIRE OF THE GREAT KHAN

and Maffeo were some of the very first Europeans Kublai had ever met. When they arrived at his court, he welcomed them and asked questions about Europe.

Eventually Kublai asked them to take a message to the pope, the head of the Catholic Church in Rome. In those days, the pope was also a powerful political leader. The Polos were to ask for two things: 1) a hundred Catholic priests who had studied math, astronomy, and other subjects; 2) some holy oil that came

POPE GREGORY X

from a special church in Jerusalem. The holy oil was rumored to have special powers, which the khan probably hoped to use against enemies.

Kublai wanted the Polos to return to China with these things. He said that if the priests could prove Christianity was the best religion of all, he might even become a Christian himself. Did he really mean it? It's true Kublai was interested in learning about different religions. But it's also possible he hoped the missionaries would help him figure out how to gain power over Christian lands.

The Polos said they would return with the things Kublai had asked for. They left China and headed home.

IF YOU LIVED IN EUROPE

- YOU WERE PROBABLY A POOR, HARDWORKING PEASANT. EVEN CHILDREN WORKED INSTEAD OF GOING TO SCHOOL. PEOPLE OFTEN GOT MARRIED WHEN THEY WERE TEENAGERS.
- YOU STUNK BECAUSE YOU DIDN'T TAKE A BATH VERY OFTEN. WHEN YOU DID BATHE, YOU MIGHT BATHE OUTDOORS IN A STREAM OR PAY TO TAKE A BATH AT A BATH-HOUSE. IF YOU WERE LUCKY, YOU HAD SOAP. YOU USED STICKS OR RAGS AS A TOOTHBRUSH. FORGET ABOUT TOOTHPASTE.
- YOU PROBABLY DIDN'T KNOW HOW TO READ OR WRITE.

AT THE TIME OF MARCO POLO

- YOUR TOILET WAS A SPECIAL POT. (IT DIDN'T FLUSH.) YOUR TOILET PAPER WAS HAY, STICKS, OR WHATEVER WAS HANDY. WHEN YOUR POT GOT FULL, YOU DUMPED THE STINKY STUFF IN THE STREET ALONG WITH OTHER GARBAGE. IF YOU LIVED IN VENICE, YOU DUMPED IT IN THE CANAL.

- YOU PROBABLY DIDN'T LIVE IN A BIG CITY LIKE MARCO DID. YOU LIVED IN A SMALL TOWN OR IN THE COUNTRY. YOUR HOUSE WAS MADE OF WOOD, STRAW, MUD BRICK, OR PLASTER. IF YOU WERE RICH, IT WAS STONE.

Chapter 2
Marco Leaves Home

By the time the Polos returned to Italy in 1269, the pope had died. They waited and waited for another pope to be chosen. Two years later, in the spring of 1271, they decided to quit waiting and head back to China.

Marco was seventeen now. He wanted to go to China, too. He didn't want to be left behind. His father and uncle knew the trip would be dangerous. Still, they agreed to take him along.

They sailed from Venice into the Adriatic Sea and then south to the Mediterranean Sea. In those days, sailors believed there were giant monsters in the sea. Maybe Niccolo thought his son would get scared and want to turn back. But Marco never did.

Their first stop was the city of Acre, then on to Jerusalem. To Christians, Jews, and Muslims, Jerusalem is a holy city. Important events in each religion took place there. Jesus lived and died in Jerusalem. King Solomon built the first Jewish temple there. And the Islamic prophet Muhammad rose to heaven in Jerusalem.

Ownership of Jerusalem has changed many times over the centuries. In 1099 armies of Christian knights conquered the city during military campaigns called the Crusades. Then in 1187, Muslims gained control of the city. Jerusalem was still under Muslim rule when the Polos stopped there and took a sample of the special oil from the church. Afterward, they set out for China.

They hadn't gone far when they heard that a new pope had finally been chosen. Luckily he was nearby, in Acre. The Polos went and told him of the khan's request for a hundred priests.

The new pope listened. He decided to send some expensive presents such as crystal. But he would send only two friars instead of priests. In a letter to the khan, the pope explained that the two friars would train Kublai's men to become priests. Then the new Mongol and Chinese priests could teach others about Christianity.

Would this change make Kublai Khan mad? The Polos hoped not. They needed the khan's friendship in order to make sure no one in his empire harmed them. That way, they could buy Chinese goods and safely bring them all the way back to Europe.

In China, they not only planned to get silks, but they wanted to bring back porcelain, too. Porcelain is a kind of pottery that is made from special white clay and painted with beautiful designs.

TO CHINA BY LAND AND SEA

IN MARCO POLO'S DAY, THERE
WERE TWO MAIN WAYS TO GET TO
EAST ASIA FROM EUROPE: THE SILK
ROAD AND THE SPICE ROUTE.
NEITHER WAY WAS EASY. THE
SILK ROAD WAS ABOUT FIVE
THOUSAND MILES LONG,
MOSTLY OVER LAND. THE
SPICE ROUTE WAS MOSTLY
BY SEA. EACH WAS NAMED
FOR THE THINGS EUROPEANS WANTED MOST FROM
ASIA: SILK AND SPICES.

A TRADER USUALLY ONLY TRAVELED PARTWAY
ON THESE ROUTES. WHEN HE REACHED A CITY, HE

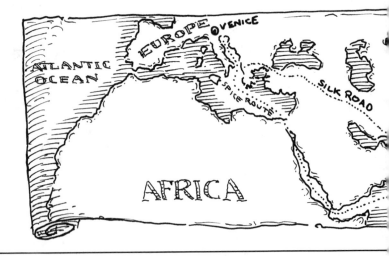

SOLD HIS GOODS (WOOD, FOR EXAMPLE) TO ANOTHER MERCHANT THERE. THAT MERCHANT TOOK THE WOOD FARTHER ALONG THE ROUTE TO ANOTHER CITY, WHERE IT WAS SOLD AGAIN. THE GOODS CHANGED HANDS MANY TIMES BEFORE REACHING CHINA, WHERE THE WOOD WAS TRADED FOR SILKS AND SPICES. AT THIS POINT, THE RETURN TRIP BEGAN.

BOTH COMING AND GOING, EACH TRADER CHARGED A LITTLE MORE FOR THE RESOLD GOODS. AFTER ALL, THEY WANTED TO MAKE A PROFIT. BY THE TIME THE GOODS GOT TO THE END OF THE JOURNEY, THEY COST MUCH MORE THAN WHEN THEY STARTED OUT.

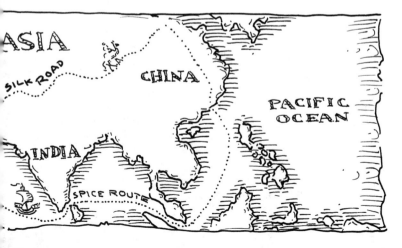

In other parts of Kublai's empire, the Polos hoped to find diamonds, rubies, and pearls. In Turkey, they would buy lovely carpets. They wanted spices such as nutmeg, cinnamon, and pepper from India and the Spice Islands (now called Indonesia). Back home, they could sell everything and get rich.

In November of 1271, the Polos and the two friars set off for China again. First, they sailed north in the Mediterranean Sea. When

they tried to land in Armenia, they ran into trouble. Egyptians were attacking it.

The two friars got scared. The trip had barely begun and already there was danger. So they turned back. The Polos continued on. But now all they had was holy oil to take to the khan!

THE SILK SECRET

THE CHINESE MADE BEAUTIFUL CLOTHES OUT OF SILK FABRIC. DESIGNS WERE SEWN ON THE SILK WITH BRIGHTLY COLORED THREAD. THEY WERE WORKS OF ART! FOR THOUSANDS OF YEARS, SILK PRODUCERS IN CHINA KEPT THEIR WAYS OF MAKING SILK A SECRET. EVENTUALLY, THEIR SECRET GOT OUT. HERE'S HOW SILK IS MADE:

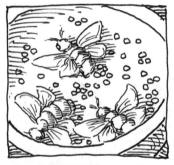

1) SILKWORM MOTHS LAY EGGS.

2) AFTER TEN DAYS, THE EGGS HATCH INTO SMALL CATERPILLARS CALLED SILKWORMS.

3) THE SILKWORMS EAT MULBERRY LEAVES.

4) WHEN A SILKWORM IS ABOUT ONE MONTH OLD, IT SHOOTS A STREAM OF LIQUID FROM ITS MOUTH. THIS HARDENS INTO A STRAND OF SILK. THE WORM WRAPS THE STRAND AROUND ITSELF, CREATING A COCOON. THE COCOON IS MADE OF A SINGLE THREAD THAT CAN BE A HALF MILE LONG!

5) SILK WORKERS DROP THE COCOONS INTO BOILING WATER TO KILL THE PUPA. OTHERWISE, THE MOTH PUPA MIGHT BITE ITS WAY OUT OF THE COCOON AND BREAK THE SILK STRAND. BOILING ALSO MAKES THE SILK SOFT AND EASY TO UNWIND.

6) THE COCOONS ARE UNWOUND BY HAND.

7) THREE OR MORE STRANDS OF SILK ARE TWISTED TOGETHER TO MAKE ONE STRONG THREAD.

8) THE THREADS ARE WOVEN INTO SILK CLOTH AND THEN DYED BRIGHT COLORS.

Chapter 3
The Long Trip to China

On the way to China, Marco saw sights that seemed very strange to him. He wrote about them in journals. Because he was a merchant, he paid special attention to the products of each area. He also noted any dangers, and whether food and water were easy to find. Maybe he thought this information would help other merchants who traveled to Asia after him.

One of the first and most famous sights he saw was Mount Ararat in what is now Turkey. According to the Bible, this was where Noah's ark landed after a great flood. Deep snow covered the mountaintop all year round. So Marco saw no point in going up there to try to find the ark.

Near the Caspian Sea, Marco saw natural oil wells for the first time. It was the kind of oil used to make gasoline today. In Europe at that time, people burned fires, candles, or oils made from animals or vegetables for light. Marco was amazed that the oil he saw in Asia came from the ground. He called it "a fountain from which oil springs."

In Persia (called Iran now), Marco saw three famous tombs. They were said to be the tombs of the three wise men who came to see the baby Jesus. Marco wrote that the three wise men were "buried in three large and beautiful monuments side by side."

Plans constantly changed during the long trip. The Polos were attacked by bandits in Persia, but they managed to escape. To avoid more run-ins with bandits, they decided to head south for the Indian Ocean. Maybe sea travel would be safer.

They searched for ships in the city of Hormuz along the Persian Gulf. This was a great trading center where merchants from India came to sell spices, pearls, silk, and ivory. Marco said that sometimes a wind blew there that was "so hot that it would kill everybody." When the people of Hormuz heard this wind coming, they jumped into the nearest stream until it passed.

Unfortunately the ships in Hormuz were poorly built. They were held together with rope made from coconut husks, instead of nails. The Polos decided that traveling overland might be safer after all!

The Polos turned around and headed north toward the land that is now Afghanistan. There, they saw a fabulous ruby mine. They saw wild sheep with  curly horns five feet long. These sheep were later named *Ovis poli*, which means "Polo's sheep."

Marco had been sick for a while at this point. He heard a legend that said breathing fresh air in the mountains of Afghanistan would cure any illness. After resting up in those mountains he did get well, and they moved on.

There were many other interesting sights in Afghanistan. In the city of Balkh, Marco wrote to watch out for lions. In Shibarghan he found "the very best melons in the world." The mountains of Talikan were made of salt, which was "so hard it could only be broken with iron picks." Marco thought there was enough salt there to "supply the whole world to the end of time." Salt was worth a lot back then, so he was impressed.

The Polos had gone five thousand miles by the time they arrived in the city of Lop. But before they reached Kublai Khan's palace, they would have to cross the dangerous Gobi Desert. This desert covers five hundred thousand square miles in northern China and southern Mongolia. It has sand mountains called dunes that rise as high as

1,250 feet. That's as tall as the Empire State Building in New York (minus its antenna)!

In Lop, the Polos bought food and lots of water. They hired camels, which were called "ships of the desert." If necessary, a camel can go without water for up to two weeks and without food for even longer. Its wide feet stop it from sinking deep into the sand. Its strong jaws allow it to eat thorny desert plants. Long eyelashes keep sand from blowing in its eyes. It can even close its nostrils to keep sand out of its nose.

The Polos rode through the desert at night because the days were too hot. The Gobi's sandstorms can kill travelers.

About once a day, they stopped at an oasis (oh-AY-siss) to rest and buy more supplies. An oasis is a spot in the desert with a spring of underground water. Small villages had formed around the Gobi's oases.

Marco heard strange sounds in the desert that sounded like people marching, talking, and playing drums. According to legend, it was an army of ghosts. Sometimes people chased after the

ghosts, got lost, and died. The sounds were really caused by strong winds and shifting sands.

It took the Polos a month to cross six hundred miles of the Gobi Desert. In his palace in the city of Shang-tu, Kublai Khan got word that the Polos were returning. (Shang-tu is in the Hebei province of modern-day China.) He sent guides to bring them to his palace. And so, on the Polos went, through what are now the provinces of Gansu, Shaanxi, Shanxi, and Ningxia Hai.)

After so long a journey, Marco may have wondered if he'd ever meet the powerful Mongol leader he'd heard so much about.

Chapter 4
The Great Kublai Khan

A few days later, the Polos arrived at the palace in Shang-tu. After three and a half years of traveling, Marco finally met Kublai Khan.

Marco wrote that "there was great rejoicing at the Court because of their arrival." They "met with attention and honour from everybody." The khan was happy about the pope's letters and gifts. He was glad to see the Polos and wasn't angry that no priests had come with them.

Marco was twenty-one years old at the time. The khan was nearly three times his age. Marco said he had black eyes, pale skin, and was of medium height. He was very impressed by the khan's riches and palaces.

KUBLAI KHAN

The khan's summer palace at Shang-tu was made of white marble. It was decorated with gold and surrounded by a sixteen-mile wall.

WINTER PALACE

Inside the walls there were beautiful gardens where ten thousand white horses grazed. Ten thousand horses? According to Marco, there were. Kublai rode his horse around the park, followed by another horse with a pet leopard on its back.

During winter, the khan lived in another palace. It was located just north of what is now Beijing, which is the capital of the People's

Republic of China today. The Polos visited the winter palace, too. Its rooms were decorated with golden sculptures and paintings of dragons, beasts, knights, and birds. Its dining room was big enough for six thousand guests . . . at least, that's what Marco said. Other rooms contained rich treasures that no one but the khan was allowed to see.

Around the palace there was a beautiful park full of deer, gazelles, and other animals. Whenever Kublai saw an interesting tree somewhere in his empire, he had elephants drag it to this park so he could plant it there. Mile-long walls with guard towers on each corner surrounded this palace. The biggest gate in the wall would only open for the khan himself to pass through.

Every spring, Kublai went on a hunting trip. He didn't do any hunting himself. His servants hunted while he watched from a big tent. Marco said that there were five thousand

hunting dogs and ten thousand falconers. Falconers
were men who carried falcons (large birds of prey)
that attacked other animals when released.

Kublai Khan did everything in a big way. Even his family was very big. He had four main wives and forty-seven sons. No one knows how many daughters he had.

His favorite wife was named Chabi. She helped the khan understand the customs

CHABI

of the people he ruled so he would be a better leader. Kublai had been ruler of the Mongol empire for fifteen years by the time Marco met him. (There were other khans in Asia, but Kublai was the boss of them all.)

Unlike most warriors, Kublai didn't try to force conquered people to change their religion. In fact, he did just the opposite. He told leaders of different religions that *their* religion was his favorite. That made them happy, so they didn't try to overthrow him.

Kublai Khan studied the teachings of Jesus and Buddha. He hired Muslims to work in his government. He also respected rules of a Chinese philosopher named Confucius (kuhn-FYOO-shuss) who was born in 551 B.C. Confucius taught that people should treat others as they'd like to be treated themselves. He also taught that everyone should be educated, not just rich people. This was a very unusual idea at the time.

Kublai Khan's grandfather Genghis had already conquered northern China. In 1279—four years after the Polos arrived—Kublai conquered southern China. This was his biggest military victory.

Kublai grew even richer by taxing the wealthy cities of southern China and his other new lands. Marco called him "the most powerful of men, in subjects, lands and treasures, that there is on earth."

Even though Kublai had murdered many people and grabbed their land, Marco thought he was a fair ruler. When farmers had a bad harvest, they didn't have to pay taxes. Hungry people were fed for free with corn, wheat, rice, and other grains kept in storage.

Marco wrote that Kublai Khan was: "the wisest man and the ablest in all respects, the best rule[r] of his subjects and of empire and the man of the highest character of all that have ever been in the whole history" of his people.

GENGHIS KHAN
(1162–1227)

GENGHIS KHAN WAS KUBLAI KHAN'S GRANDFATHER. HE WAS ONE OF THE MOST SKILLFUL AND FEARED MILITARY LEADERS EVER.

IN 1206, HE UNITED MONGOL NOMADS INTO AN ARMY. A YEAR LATER, HE LED THEM ON THE FIRST OF MANY BLOODY INVASIONS OF SURROUNDING VILLAGES. WITHIN FIFTY YEARS, HIS ARMY HAD CONQUERED TWO-THIRDS OF ASIA. HIS EMPIRE GREW TO INCLUDE PARTS OF RUSSIA, IRAQ, IRAN, AFGHANISTAN, AND NORTHERN CHINA.

HIS WARS WERE CRUEL AND HIS LAWS WERE STRICT. HE CLAIMED ANY TOWN HE

WANTED FOR HIS OWN. SOME-
TIMES HE STOLE ITS RICHES,
THEN BURNED IT DOWN.
PEOPLE WERE SCARED HE
WOULD KILL THEM IF THEY
PUT UP A FIGHT. SOME
SURRENDERED WITHOUT
A STRUGGLE.

AFTER HIS DEATH,
OTHER KHANS TOOK OVER
HIS CONQUERED LANDS.
EVENTUALLY KUBLAI
KHAN BECAME ONE OF
THOSE RULERS.

Chapter 5
Marco Works for the Khan

Kublai Khan liked Marco because he was smart and amusing. According to Marco, over the next seventeen years he was sent on missions to different areas of the Mongol empire.

Marco never said exactly what the khan asked him to do on any of these missions. But he did say he always did a good job.

It seems that part of his job was snooping around. After each mission, he gave the khan a report of what he'd done

and seen. These lively reports entertained Kublai. They were much more interesting than the dry facts reported back by the khan's other men. Marco took notes as he traveled. He brought interesting stories from faraway lands back to Kublai's court. He wrote that he tried to "gather knowledge of anything that would be likely to interest the khan." It seemed that Marco had a bright future working for Kublai Khan.

In his book, Marco's stories don't strike modern readers as all that entertaining. But people wrote in a much more formal style back then. One story Marco wrote about was the day he saw what he thought was a huge fifteen-foot-long snake. He said its legs each

had three claws. Its jaws could swallow a person! This turned out to be a crocodile.

Marco had never seen coal before. He was amazed to see people burning black rocks.

The Mongols had one of the very first pony express systems for sending mail. Marco was impressed by how fast Kublai could send a

message. There were ten thousand stations about thirty miles apart along the major roads throughout the khan's lands. A messenger could rest at a station, get a new pony, and continue on carrying news. Foot messengers carried a rider's news from the stations to nearby villages.

The Mongols had destroyed some cities that Marco visited. Many villages in the region of Tibet had once been beau-tiful. But when Marco got there, the people were gone.  Only tigers and other wild animals roamed the ruins, making it very dangerous!

Marco saw paper money for the first time in China. Paper had been invented in China around 105 A.D., more than a thousand years before Marco's arrival. At first, pieces of old

CHINESE PAPER MONEY

fishnet, rags, hemp, and grasses were used to make it. They were boiled until they turned mushy. Then they were flattened and dried.

Later, paper was made from bark. Marco wrote that paper money was made from the bark of "the mulberry tree, the leaves of which are the food of silkworms . . ." The bigger the piece of paper money, the more it was worth.

In most of Europe, people didn't know how to make paper during Marco's time. They didn't have paper money until the 1600s. Marco decided that paper money was better than the heavy coins used back home.

Instead of paper, European books were

Chinese Printing

DESIGNS WERE DRAWN ON PAPER, THEN CARVED INTO WOODBLOCKS. MOVABLE TYPE WAS SELECTED FROM A TRAY OF CLAY CHARACTERS AND THEN WAS ARRANGED IN AN IRON FRAME AND HELD IN PLACE BY WAX.

THE BLOCK OR FRAME WAS THEN INKED AND PRESSED ONTO PAPER TO MAKE MULTIPLE PRINTS.

handwritten on vellum or parchment. Those were made from the skin of animals such as sheep, calves, pigs, or goats. It was harder and more expensive to make than paper. The Chinese printed books and money by hand-pressing paper against ink-covered letters or pictures carved on blocks of pear-tree wood. Woodblock printing was faster than writing by hand. But it was still a slow way to make a book.

In China, Marco was surprised by the loudest bang he'd ever heard. It was the sound of gunpowder exploding. Many centuries earlier, the Chinese had invented gunpowder. But Europeans didn't know about it. In the middle 1200s, an Englishman named Roger Bacon figured out how to make gunpowder, probably after studying a Chinese firecracker. The first known gun was made in China in 1288. Guns were used in Europe as early as 1314.

Chapter 6
Fierce Mongol Warriors

Marco described many Mongol battles in his book. Some he witnessed. Others he merely heard about.

One of Kublai Khan's longest battles had ended two years before Marco arrived to write about it. It was an attack on a city along the Han River that began in 1268.

The city was built like a fort, with a wall around it. Kublai's commanders could not get inside the walls to attack. So they formed a circle around the city that was made of soldiers, ships, and a wall of dirt and mud. The people couldn't get past them to get supplies.

Kublai's commanders tried to attack the city several times. Each time there was a bloody battle, but neither side would give in. This went on for five years.

Finally, Kublai sent two engineers to help conquer the city. Outside the walls, they built tall catapults called

MANGONEL

mangonels. Mangonel (MANG-joh-nel) is based on a word that means "engine of war." It launched giant stones, darts, burning tar, and even poop over the city's walls. If an animal died from disease, they shot its body over the wall, too! They hoped to spread so much disease among the people inside that they would have to give up. And at last, they did.

Kublai tried twice, but he was never able to conquer Japan. This shocked both Europeans and Asians, who had begun to think the fierce Mongol army couldn't be defeated.

Mongols liked to stage surprise attacks whenever possible. They were quiet at first and used flags or lanterns to communicate. Sometimes they shot whistling arrows as signals to each other. When it was time for troops to attack, a commander told his musicians to beat big drums.

A Mongol warrior fought with swords, spears, axes, and even lassos. But his main weapon was his bow and quiver of hollow-reed arrows. Because

the bow was short, a soldier could easily shoot it
while riding a horse. It shot arrows twice as far as
the bows used in Europe. The Mongol bow hit its

target more often, too. However, it took greater strength to shoot an arrow from the Mongol type of bow.

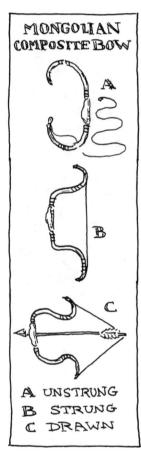

MONGOLIAN COMPOSITE BOW

A UNSTRUNG
B STRUNG
C DRAWN

EUROPEAN ARCHER

Mongol warriors were very good riders. On long trips, they each brought several ponies with short, powerful legs. When a pony got tired, its rider switched to a different one. Sometimes Mongols rode day and night. They ate and slept while riding! They were only able to conquer lands where grass grew. That's because their ponies needed grass for food.

As Kublai Khan got older, he couldn't ride anymore. In 1287 one of his relatives tried to overthrow him. Kublai and his troops went to the Liao River to fight him. But Kublai was so tired that he could only watch from a wood tower carried by four elephants as his soldiers defeated his relative.

- YOU WERE A NOMAD WHO HERDED SHEEP, GOATS, OR CATTLE.

- YOU PROBABLY LIVED IN A BIG TENT CALLED A *YURT*.

AT THE TIME OF MARCO POLO

- YOU DRANK MARE'S MILK AND ATE MEAT. YOU NEVER LIVED IN ONE PLACE LONG ENOUGH TO GROW A GARDEN, SO YOU HAD TO FIND WILD BERRIES, NUTS, AND VEGETABLES TO EAT.
- YOU PRAYED TO MANY HOUSEHOLD GODS BUT BELIEVED IN ONE SUPREME BEING.
- YOUR MOST IMPORTANT POSSESSION WAS YOUR HORSE. HORSE STEALING WAS PUNISHED BY DEATH.

Chapter 7
Trapped

Marco was now in his late thirties. He had spent half of his life in China. He, his father, and his uncle had a treasure of jewels and gold.

Kublai Khan was in his seventies by then. In those days, very few people lived that long. In his last years, the khan became ill. The Polos worried he might die.

Some Mongols were jealous of Marco because the khan liked and trusted him so much. Once Kublai died, would Marco be imprisoned or killed?

Several times over the years, the Polos had asked the khan if they could leave China. He liked having them around, so he always said no. Marco was stuck. Traveling home to Italy would have been too dangerous without the khan's protection.

But in 1291, the Polos got lucky. A seventeen-year-old Mongol princess was being sent to Persia

PRINCESS KOKACHIN

to get married. Women didn't travel alone in those days. The princess needed many guards and companions. Her guards thought a trip overland would be too hard for her. They wanted to travel by sea. Marco had just returned from a voyage to India. Since he knew the route, he would make a perfect guide.

The khan had a tough choice to make. He wanted to be sure the princess arrived safely. But he

didn't want Marco and the others to leave. However, he eventually agreed to let them guide the princess.

For the trip, Kublai gave the Polos thirteen ships with six hundred servants and crew members on board. He also gave them messages to deliver to the kings of France, England, and Spain.

To protect the travelers, Kublai gave the Polos two golden tablets. They were each about one foot long and four inches wide. A message written on them ordered everyone they met along the way to be of help. If they weren't, Kublai might see to it that they were put to death!

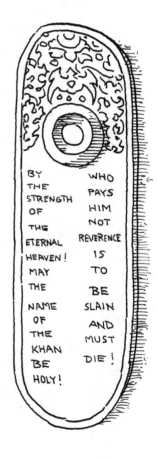

BY THE STRENGTH OF THE ETERNAL HEAVEN! MAY THE NAME OF THE KHAN BE HOLY! WHO PAYS HIM NOT REVERENCE IS TO BE SLAIN AND MUST DIE!

IF YOU WERE CHINESE

- YOUR HOUSE WAS PROBABLY BUILT OF BAMBOO AND WOOD.
- YOU ATE FOODS YOU GREW, SUCH AS RICE, WHEAT, OR SOYBEANS.
- YOUR RELIGION MAY HAVE BEEN BUDDHISM OR TAOISM. BUDDHISM BEGAN IN INDIA ABOUT 500 BC AND THEN SPREAD TO CHINA. BUDDHISM TAUGHT THAT A WELL-BALANCED LIFE WOULD HELP A PERSON FIND HAPPINESS. THE TAOIST

AT THE TIME OF MARCO POLO

RELIGION BEGAN IN CHINA ABOUT TWENTY-FIVE HUNDRED YEARS AGO. THE WORD *TAO* MEANS "PATH." TAI CHI CHUAN IS AN EXERCISE OF THE MIND AND BODY THAT IS LARGELY BASED ON TAOIST TEACHINGS.

BUDDHA

• YOU RESPECTED THE TEACHINGS OF THE PHILOSOPHER CONFUCIUS.

Chapter 8
Delivering the Princess Bride

Kublai's golden tablets acted almost like a magic charm, protecting the Polos as they traveled homeward. Marco later wrote that throughout the khan's lands they "were supplied with horses and provisions" and "given two hundred horsemen" to escort them and ensure their safety from one district to another.

The Polos sailed through the China Sea, past Vietnam. Heavy rains called monsoons forced them to land on the island of Sumatra. They stayed there for five months. Cannibals—people who ate human flesh—tried to attack them.

Marco was amazed by the unusual things he saw in Sumatra. In his journals he wrote that

he tasted a nut he said was "the size of a man's head." It was a coconut.

He wrote that he saw a unicorn. A unicorn is a mythical animal. It is said to be white, with a long white horn sticking out of its forehead. What Marco actually saw was a rhinoceros.

He also claimed he saw small, hairy apelike "people" called orang pendeks. Were these creatures real? No one knows for sure. However, even today some people claim to have found bits of their fur.

On the island of Sri Lanka near the southern tip of India, Marco met a king who owned the biggest ruby in the world. It was as long as the palm of his hand and as big around as his arm.

Along the coast of India, they saw divers hunting for pearls. Merchants hired the divers. They also hired magicians to cast a spell on

the ocean. The spell supposedly kept the divers from getting eaten by sharks.

Their sea voyage took twenty-six months—more than two years. By the time Marco landed in Hormuz, all but eight of their six hundred crewmen were dead. He never explained how they died, so no one knows what happened to them. They probably died from disease, storms, or attacks by pirates and bandits. Or maybe there never had been six hundred crewmen to start with.

When they finally docked in Persia, there was bad news. The princess's fiancé was dead. Nevertheless, a wedding took place. The princess married his son instead.

Then came even worse news. The great Kublai Khan had also died. Now Marco could never return to China. Without the khan's protection, traveling in Asia was not safe.

The Polos headed for Venice, traveling by camel, ship, and on foot. In Turkey, they were robbed. Marco didn't tell how much of their

riches were lost. He also did not tell why it took over a year to go such a short distance.

Altogether it took them three and a half years to travel from China to Italy. Today this trip can be made by airplane in less than a day!

Chapter 9
Home Again

When the Polos finally arrived home in 1295, their families didn't recognize them. After all, they had been gone from Venice for twenty-four years.

Their skin was darkly tanned from the desert sun. Their clothes were dirty and ragged. They looked nothing like rich merchants. Some people didn't believe they really *were* the Polos.

A few days after their return, there was a feast. Once everyone had eaten, the Polos brought out the clothes they had worn on the way home from China. They ripped the seams with knives. Rubies, diamonds, and other jewels fell out!

Although people now believed they were the Polos, not everyone believed the tales of their

travels. Marco's stories seemed wild to people who had never been outside of Italy. For instance, when he claimed he had seen a unicorn, other Venetians laughed at him.

Soon, Marco settled back into life as a merchant. It probably wasn't as exciting as working for the khan.

Almost immediately, war broke out between Venice and another Italian city-state called Genoa. These two city-states had a history of fighting. Both wanted to be the most powerful in Europe.

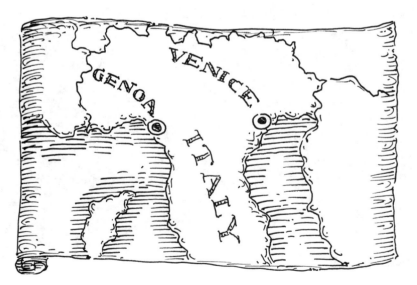

Marco became the "gentleman commander" of a Venetian ship. This sounds like an important title. But a more experienced captain was really in charge.

In 1298 ships from Genoa sailed southward around the boot of Italy and then turned northward into the Adriatic Sea. They planned to attack Venice's navy, the biggest in Europe. They had started out with about ninety-four ships. Sixteen ships had been lost in a storm along the way.

Venice heard that Genoa's navy was coming. They sent ninety-five ships to fight them.

The two navies met in the Adriatic Sea. For a while, it looked like Venice would win. But then all sixteen of Genoa's lost ships showed up to join the fight. Venice's ships were defeated in just one day. Genoa's navy captured about seven thousand Venetians—including Marco!

SEA BATTLES

IN THE THIRTEENTH CENTURY, GENOA AND
VENICE BOTH HAD MIGHTY NAVIES. THEY TRAVELED
THE SEAS IN WOODEN SHIPS CALLED *GALLEYS*.
A GALLEY WAS NARROW, USUALLY ABOUT ONE
HUNDRED FIFTY FEET LONG BUT ONLY SIXTEEN TO
TWENTY-FIVE FEET WIDE. IT HAD A FEW SAILS BUT
WAS MOSTLY MAN-POWERED.

A HUNDRED OR SO OARSMEN SAT ON BENCHES
THAT WERE SET IN ROWS ALONG EACH SIDE OF
THE GALLEY. THREE MEN SAT ON EACH BENCH.
EACH MAN ROWED A DIFFERENT OAR THAT WAS
ABOUT THIRTY FEET LONG. THEY HAD TO BE GOOD
AT THEIR JOBS, SO THEIR OARS DIDN'T BUMP INTO
EACH OTHER.

SIX DOCTORS MIGHT BE ON A GALLEY, BUT THERE
WAS ONLY ONE COOK! THERE WERE AS MANY AS
TWENTY MUSICIANS. DURING A BATTLE, THEY BANGED
DRUMS AND TOOTED TRUMPETS, HOPING TO SCARE
THE ENEMY.

A GALLEY CREW WORE HELMETS AND ARMOR AND
FOUGHT WITH SPEARS, SWORDS, AND CROSSBOWS.
THEY SHOT ARROWS LIT WITH FIRE AT AN ENEMY
SHIP'S SAILS. SOMETIMES THEY THREW A POWDER
CALLED LIME AT ENEMY SOLDIERS TO BURN THEIR
EYES AND SKIN.

IT WAS MORE THAN ONE HUNDRED YEARS AFTER
MARCO'S DEATH THAT SHIPS FIRST HAD CANNONS.

Chapter 10
The Famous Book

Marco was put in a Genoa jail for about ten months. There wasn't much to do, and the other Venetian prisoners were probably bored. Luckily, Marco was a good storyteller. He entertained them with tales of his travels.

An author named Rustichello was in the same jail as Marco. He thought Marco's stories were interesting. He offered to help turn them into a book. It was a good way to pass the time. The two men began writing.

Marco told his stories aloud while Rustichello wrote them down. Marco couldn't remember everything. He decided he needed the journals he'd written in Asia. So his father sent them to the jail.

No one knows how much Rustichello changed Marco's stories. The book is written in different styles, probably depending on which of the two men was writing a particular part. Other books Rustichello had written before were adventure stories about noble knights. It's likely that Rustichello tried to make Marco's stories extra-dramatic. After Venice and Genoa signed a peace treaty in 1299,

Marco was set free. He returned to Venice with the book he and Rustichello had written.

Marco titled his book *The Description of the World*. Later, it was called *The Travels of Marco Polo*. It was divided into an introduction plus four main parts.

The introduction told readers about the Polos making two trips to China and meeting Kublai Khan. Part One was about Marco's trip across Asia toward China. Part Two described Kublai's empire. Part Three was about Japan (which Marco never visited) and Marco's trip home from China to Venice. Part Four wasn't really about his travels. It described Mongol wars.

In his book, Marco didn't write much about everyday things, conversations he had, or friends he'd made in Asia. These things would be very interesting to readers today, but Marco didn't think readers of his day would care about such information.

The Travels of Marco Polo is mostly a geography

book, telling about the lands the Polos visited. Just fifty-five years after he died, Marco's book was used to help create a famous world map.

The original version Marco and Rustichello wrote in jail has never been found. No one knows how many copies of the book were made. In Marco's day, books were handwritten by monks in monasteries using goose-quill pens. It took between three months and three years to make a beautifully illustrated book. So there weren't many books around.

About one hundred fifty handwritten copies of the book are now in museums and other collections. No two are exactly alike.

A good printing press wasn't invented until the 1440s. In 1477 Marco's popular book was machine-printed for the first time. The first copies were in the German language. Soon the book was reprinted in

English, Spanish, and almost every other language in Europe. No wonder Marco Polo became famous! The book is still in print. Copies can be found in many libraries today.

GUTENBERG'S NEW PRINTING PRESS

ABOUT 120 YEARS AFTER MARCO DIED, A GERMAN
NAMED JOHANNES GUTENBERG (CIRCA 1390-1468)
INVENTED A NEW WAY OF PRINTING. HE CREATED A
DIFFERENT KIND OF PRESS THAT USED SEPARATE
METAL LETTERS TO FORM WORDS AND SENTENCES.
BEFORE GUTENBERG, AN ENTIRE PIECE OF TEXT
WOULD BE ENGRAVED ON A PIECE OF METAL CALLED
A PLATE AND ALL THE WORDS WOULD BE PRINTED
TOGETHER AT ONCE. IT WAS A VERY TIME CONSUM-
ING PROCESS. AND NONE OF THE INDIVIDUAL WORDS
IN THE TEXT COULD EVER BE USED SEPARATELY. BUT
GUTENBERG'S INDIVIDUAL LETTERS WERE USED TO
MAKE UP WORDS THAT COULD BE SET UP QUICKLY IN
LINES TO FORM A PAGE. THE LETTERS WERE REUS-
ABLE.

THE FIRST BOOKS HE PRODUCED ON HIS PRESS
WERE BIBLES. HE BEGAN PRINTING THEM IN 1452.
AFTER THE PAGES WERE PRINTED, HE SENT THEM TO
A BINDERY. THERE, THEY WERE GLUED AND STITCHED
TOGETHER ALONG ONE SIDE TO FORM A BOOK.

BECAUSE OF GUTENBERG, MORE BOOKS WERE
PUBLISHED IN THE FOLLOWING 50 YEARS THAN HAD
BEEN PRODUCED IN THE PREVIOUS 1,000 YEARS. ONCE
BOOKS WERE CHEAPER AND EASIER TO GET, MORE
PEOPLE LEARNED TO READ.

Each time Marco's book was copied, some words were changed. Sometimes that was by mistake. Mistakes were especially easy to make when the book was translated into another language. Other times, the scribe or printer changed Marco's story on purpose. For instance, when the book was translated into Irish, the printer knew his readers liked exciting stories. He made changes he thought they would like.

Chapter 11
Were Marco's Stories True?

Most historians think Marco Polo did go to China with his father and uncle. The real question is: How much of what he claimed to see and do was stretching the truth—what we call "tall tales"?

In his book, he used large numbers to describe amounts, sizes, and distances. He said the Chinese city of Hangchow had twelve thousand bridges, but it had far fewer. He said that Kublai sent an army of 360,000 horsemen and 100,000 troops to fight his enemies in 1287. But there wasn't enough food near the battlefield for so many troops, nor enough grass to feed that many horses.

Most people who first read Marco's stories had never traveled far from home. They didn't know much about the world. To them, Marco's stories about strange lands and people seemed too incredible to believe.

They decided that the book was nothing but a million lies. This helped earn him the nickname "Marco Millions." For a while, another phrase for an exaggeration was a "marco polo." At carnivals, clown puppets nicknamed Marco Millions told wild stories full of exaggeration to make the crowds laugh.

Some of Marco's stories really *were* wild. He claimed there were magicians in Kublai Khan's empire who could make glasses of wine fly. He said they could change day into night and could also turn a sunny day into a rainy one.

Today, some people wonder why he didn't write about the Great Wall of China in his book. Maybe it didn't amaze him. Much of it had been destroyed by the 1200s. It

THE GREAT WALL

was rebuilt and lengthened when the Ming family ruled China from 1368 to 1644.

People also wonder why his book doesn't mention the Chinese custom of tea drinking. This may be because tea was most popular in southern China. Marco spent most of his time in northern China.

Marco wrote that he was the governor of a Chinese city named Yang-chou for three years. Yet he never described his job. Most historians don't think he learned to speak Chinese.

Therefore it's hard to believe that Kublai chose him to govern a Chinese city.

In China, historians kept careful records. But a government worker named Polo is only mentioned once. If Marco worked for the khan for seventeen years, why wasn't he mentioned more often? Did he use a Chinese name most of the time? Maybe, but it's odd that there is no record of the arrival of three Europeans in China in the 1200s.

And what happened to the jewels Marco supposedly brought home? In 1300—five years after his return from China—he got married at age forty-five. He and his wife, Donata Badoer, eventually had three daughters: Fantina, Bellela, and Moreta. When he died he didn't leave his family a great fortune. That makes his stories about going to China seem false. But a list of his belongings around the time of his death suggests that he did leave behind one of Kublai Khan's gold tablets. That makes his stories seem true. Where else would he have gotten something like that, except from the khan himself? Could he have bought it, stolen it, or had a fake tablet made?

Whatever the case, Marco's book spurred on other explorers. Christopher Columbus studied it and made notes on the pages. He longed to reach China by a quicker route than Marco Polo had found. He sailed west from Spain in 1492 hoping

to find China. He didn't realize that North America and South America blocked his way.

Vasco de Gama was also very interested in the book. Eventually, he found a new sea route from Europe to Asia by sailing around the southern tip of Africa in 1497. The Silk Road wasn't used as much after that.

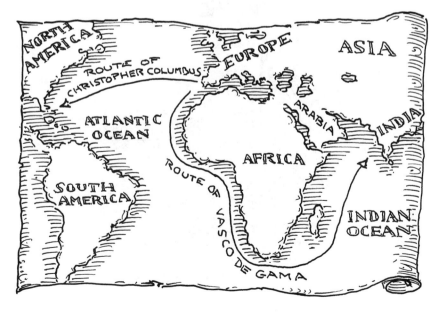

Marco was sixty-nine years old when he died in 1324. At that time, most people had decided he had made up the stories in his book. As he was dying, his friends begged him to confess the truth and say that he'd been lying. He refused. His answer to them is now famous. He told them, "I never told half of what I saw."

TIMELINE OF MARCO POLO'S LIFE

1254 — Marco Polo is born in Venice, Italy

1260 — Kublai Khan becomes ruler of the Mongol empire

1271 — Marco, his father, and his uncle leave Venice, heading for China

1275 — Marco meets Kublai Khan at his summer palace

1291 — Kublai sends Marco, his father, and his uncle to escort a princess to Persia (present-day Iran)

1294 — Kublai Khan dies on February 18

1295 — The Polos arrive back home in Venice

1298 — Marco is captured in a sea battle and imprisoned; Rustichello helps him write his book

1299 — Marco is released from prison

1300 — Marco's father dies; Marco gets married

1324 — Marco dies in Venice at age sixty-nine on January 8

1477 — About one hundred fifty years after Marco dies, copies of his book are printed on Johannes Gutenberg's new printing press

TIMELINE OF THE WORLD

Mongols destroy the city of Baghdad — **1258**

Italian artist Giotto is born — **1267**

Pope Clement IV dies — **1268**

Germans invent the spinning wheel — **1280**

The first gun is made in China — **1288**

The end of the Crusades — **1291**

A long drought causes the Anasazi Native Americans to — **1300**
abandon their cliff dwellings at Mesa Verde, Colorado

An Italian author named Dante Alighieri begins writing his — **1308**
famous book *The Divine Comedy*

Wang Zhen of China develops new printing techniques using — **1313**
sixty thousand Chinese characters carved from wood

Aztecs begin building their capital city in Mexico — **1320**

Twenty-three years after Marco dies, a plague called the — **1347**
Black Death spreads and will eventually kill one-third
of the people in Europe

BIBLIOGRAPHY

Gardiner, Robert (editor). **The Age of the Galley.** Naval Institute Press, Maryland, 1995.

Krensky, Stephen. **Breaking into Print.** Little, Brown and Company, New York, 1996.

Larner, John. **Marco Polo and the Discovery of the World.** Yale University Press, Connecticut, 1999.

MacDonald, Fiona. **Marco Polo: A Journey Through China.** Franklin Watts, Connecticut, 1997.

Otfinoski, Steven. **Marco Polo: To China and Back.** Benchmark Books, New York, 2003.

Polo, Marco. Translated and edited by Colonel Sir Henry Yule. **The Book of Ser Marco Polo, Volumes 1 and 2**. John Murray, London, 1929.

Ross, Jr., Frank. **Oracle Bones, Stars, and Wheelbarrows.** Houghton Mifflin Company, Massachusetts, 1982.

Rossabi, Morris. **Khubilai Khan: His Life and Times.** University of California Press, California, 1988.